CONTEMPORARY SCENES
FOR YOUNG WOMEN
1985-2000

CONTEMPORARY SCENES
FOR YOUNG WOMEN
1985-2000

Edited by Shaun McKenna

OBERON BOOKS
LONDON

First published in 2000 in association with the London Academy of Music and Dramatic Art, by Oberon Books Ltd (incorporating Absolute Classics) 521 Caledonian Road, London N7 9RH Tel: 020 7607 3637/Fax: 020 7607 3629 e-mail: oberon.books@btinternet.com www.oberonbooks.com

A catalogue record for this book is available from the British Library.

ISBN: 1 84002 130 6

Cover photograph: John Haynes – taken from the 2002 LAMDA production of *Suburbia* by Eric Bogosiun

Cover design: Joe Ewart

Printed in Great Britain by Antony Rowe Ltd, Chippenham

INTRODUCTION

This collection of scenes for women contains material suitable for actresses in their mid-teens and early twenties, and is ideal for auditions, festivals and LAMDA examinations. Each extract has been specially selected for its effectiveness and coherence as a scene in isolation from the original play. Every speech is annotated with notes on the character's age, situation, and any accent or dialect that might be required. The spelling and punctuation of the stage directions, as well as the speeches themselves, have been reproduced as they appeared in their original form. The date of the first performance or publication and the international standard book number have also been included.

Whilst the selections have been made with actresses under the age of 25 in mind, this does not always mean that the characters fall into that age group. Some performers may wish to spread their wings and tackle something which might be out of their age-range. It is for this reason that some of the characters range up to their thirties. The collection, for ease of reference, has been divided into three sections, and the division has been made on the basis of the age of the character, not necessarily the age of the performer.

Contemporary plays often deal with controversial and sexual issues – and find expression in "bad language". This can present some difficulty for teachers looking for suitable material for teenagers. In this selection, these have been kept to a minimum, although some of the plays from which the speeches are taken may contain rather stronger material.

Shaun McKenna

PUBLISHERS' ADDRESSES

Amber Lane Press
Cheorl House
Church Street
Charlbury OX7 3PR
Tel: 01608 810024
Fax: 01608 810024

Faber & Faber Ltd
3 Queen Square
London WC1N 3AU
Tel: 020 7465 0045
Fax: 020 7465 0034

The Gallery Press
Loughcrew
Oldcastle
County Meath, Ireland
Tel: 00 353 49 854 1779
Fax: 00 353 49 854 1779

Nick Hern Books
The Glass House
49a Goldhawk Road
London W12 8QP
Tel: 020 8749 4953
Fax: 020 8746 2006

Oberon Books Ltd
521 Caledonian Road
London N7 9RH
Telephone: 020 7607 3637
Fax: 020 7607 3629

Warner/Chappell Plays
Third Floor
Griffin House
161 Hammersmith Road
London W6 8BS
Tel: 020 8563 5800
Fax: 020 8563 5801

Warner Books
Brettenham House
Lancaster Place
London WC2E 7EN
Tel: 020 7911 8000
Fax: 020 7911 8100

CONTENTS

PART THREE: THIRTIES

PART ONE: TEENS

INVISIBLE FRIENDS

by Alan Ayckbourn

Invisible Friends was first produced at the Stephen Joseph Theatre in the Round, Scarborough in November 1989.

The play concerns Lucy Baines, a girl in her early teens, who lives with her parents and brother Gary. Lucy has an excessive love of orderliness. The play concerns her adventures when her invisible friend, Zara, becomes visible. This speech is addressed to the audience and describes the moments leading up to Zara's first appearance.

Accent: any.

LUCY: It was the thunder that woke me. There was
a terrible storm outside now and I suddenly felt rather
frightened – and I turned to look for Zara but she wasn't
on the bed any more. She'd gone. Zara had gone. And
now there was lightning… And more thunder. And
I went to turn on my light. (*She tries her light switch.*)
Only it wasn't working. For some reason, the lights
weren't working. It must have been the storm. And
I opened my door to go and see Mum and Dad… (*She
does this.*) But as I did this, above the storm, I heard
something – someone moving downstairs. And I thought
at first it might have been Gary – he's always getting up
in the night for a sandwich – but I listened at his door –

She does so.

And I heard him snoring. It would take more than
a storm to wake Gary. And I heard the sound again,
coming from what sounded like the kitchen. And
I knew then that it must be Zara. Zara was down there.
And I knew she wanted me. And I knew she might be
frightened, too. (*She gropes her way to the stairs.*) And I felt
my way to the stairs in the dark, trying not to wake
anyone. (*Calling softly.*) Zara! Zara! Where are you? Zara!

It's me, Lucy. Don't be frightened. (*To audience.*) And then it happened. I was halfway down the stairs when – there was this tremendous flash of lightning and this huge clap of thunder and I must have caught my foot on the stairs in the dark because the next thing I knew I was falling… falling…

She falls downstairs. As she does so, with a cry…

ZARA!

Available in *Alan Ayckbourn: Plays 2*, published by Faber & Faber Ltd. Reprinted by kind permission of the publisher.

ISBN: 0 571 19457 5.

THE CHAMPION OF PARIBANOU

by Alan Ayckbourn

The Champion of Paribanou was first performed at the Stephen
Joseph Theatre in the Round, Scarborough in November 1996.

*This play for children is set in the mythical and mystical East. It
deals with questions of good and evil. Prince Ahmed is in love with
Murganah, the vizier's tomboyish daughter. Princess Nouronnihar
has been ordered by her father to marry Ahmed or one of his brothers.
As none of them want the match, they have formed a plot to gain
time. Each of the princes is to go on a quest to bring back a gift
to Nouronnihar, which she will subsequently reject. Ahmed's quest
leads him to the Mountain of Storms.   Here he meets Paribanou,
a young maiden, who tells him her story in the following speech.*

Accent: any.

PARIBANOU: Sit down. We have much to talk about.
But first I must explain a little. Do you like fairy
tales, Ahmed?

Listen to this one. And pay attention. Once upon a time
there were two children. A sister and a brother. Their
mother had died when they were very young and as
a result the brother's behaviour was often very wild.
They were brought up by their father, a good and
powerful wizard in the most happy of kingdoms. One
day it happened that their father had to leave them in
order to make a journey. He left them in the care of the
servants and before he went he bade them to be good
and well-behaved during his absence. If they were good,
he said, when he returned he would reward them with
wonderful gifts. And it happened that whilst he was
away, although the daughter obeyed her father, the
brother did not. Instead he meddled with his father's
spell books and not only tormented his sister but was
cruel to the servants. In fact, he became so wild and

uncontrollable that when the father returned the palace
was all but in ruins. For by then the son, in his search for
wealth and power, had sold his very soul to Schaibar
himself…

Schaibar, the Stranger from the Darkness who seeks to
lead us all into that same Darkness. Anyway, the wizard
could do nothing, realising he had lost his only son
forever. And he became first sad and then angry with his
daughter for just feebly standing by and doing nothing
to stop her brother. And her punishment was to remain in
a beautiful but lonely cave high on a mountain. A prison
she could never leave until she learnt to stand up for
what is right and to oppose all that is bad. Alone with
only Nasuh for company. You are the first visitor this
place has ever seen, Ahmed. Welcome.

Maybe you were sent? Who knows?

Available in *Alan Ayckbourn: Plays 2*, published by Faber &
Faber Ltd. Reprinted by kind permission of the publisher.

ISBN: 0 571 19457 5.

SEA URCHINS

by Sharman Macdonald

Sea Urchins was first produced at the Dundee Rep Theatre in May 1998, a co-production between the Tron Theatre Company and the Dundee Rep Theatre.

The play is set in the summer of 1961 on the wild Welsh coast. Rena, a Scottish girl of 11, is on holiday with her family and struggling with the pains of growing up. She indulges in a fantasy correspondence with a multiple murderer, Manning, who is on the run from the police and whose story fills the newspapers. This speech is addressed to the (unseen) murderer and concerns a 12-year-old girl, Noelle, whom Rena has met on the beach.

Accent: Scottish.

RENA: (*Whispers.*) Dear Mr Manning. Dear, dear, dear Mr Manning. I've a candidate for murder I want to introduce you to. I've got your number nine sitting in a fresh water stream in Wales waiting to have your knife plunge into her guts. Dear Mr Manning please don't take any other applications. This is important. Noelle Williams is the one for you. Please get yourself down here by the quickest method of travel. I'll reimburse any expenses you incur though it may take me a while. Girls can be bad bitches Mr Manning but Noelle Williams takes the biscuit. She'll make an awful woman when she comes to maturity. You'd be doing the world a favour were you to cease her being. About dinner time should suit. We'll all be gathered. You'll know the bitch by her yellow swimsuit and the rolls of fat on her upper arms. And the three necklace of Venus lines that circle her dark neck. She says they're a promise of the beauty that is to come. Don't go confusing the two of us. There's some maintain we look alike. I have no necklace of Venus round my neck as Noelle kindly pointed out last year. I have a red swimsuit, Mr Manning. Just so you know. It clashes with

my hair but my mother says be brazen and be damned.
She bought me the swimsuit. If only you were God, Mr
Manning. If you were God I would ask you to let me
sing so that I could join them. I'm all alone here Mr
Manning. My Father would forgive me the guitar if
I could sing. Noelle can sing. And Rhiannon. I can hear
it. I dream it, Mr Manning. I dream it so hard that when
I wake up I can taste it. My own voice and it's lovely.
Then I open up my mouth. And the sound that I hear.
Mr Manning, it's an abomination. And it hurts my heart.
Kill Noelle for me please. She only has to look at me.
She knows all my misery. She knows it better than I do
myself. That's not a thing any person should have to
suffer. So you just kill her. We're all here on earth for
a purpose. Your purpose is to rid the world of Noelle
Williams and make me happy. No-one's all bad Mr
Manning. You do this death for me. It'll be your good
deed. It'll get you into Heaven.

Available in *Sea Urchins*, published by Faber & Faber Ltd.
Reprinted by kind permission of the publisher.

ISBN: 0 571 19695 1.

BOLD GIRLS

by Rona Munro

Bold Girls was commissioned by 7:84 Scottish People's Theatre and first performed at the Cumbernauld Theatre, Strathclyde in September 1990, subsequently touring widely.

The play is set in Belfast in 1990, against the background of the Troubles. Deirdre is 15, a disturbed young girl who has been hanging around outside the home of Marie Donnelly, a widow whose husband was killed by the British army. In this speech, Deirdre reveals why she has 'infiltrated' Marie's family. She believes Marie's late husband, Michael, to be her father, and that she was conceived during his marriage to Marie. Marie has just discovered that Michael had also been having an affair with her best friend, Cassie. Deirdre once saw Michael and Cassie making love in a car.

Accent: Belfast.

DEIRDRE: He was my Daddy.

He was. He was my Daddy.

My Mum told me.

She said my Dad was a bad man, and for years I thought my Daddy was a hood, then she told me he was a bad man because he left her, left her flat with me on the way and I thought that didn't make him bad because didn't I want to leave her too? So I started asking.

No-one will tell you the truth to your face. But I heard his name, so I went looking for him. I used to follow him about. That's how I saw him with her. In his car. She was wearing a bright red dress with no back to it, that made me stare first you know because I couldn't imagine how she could stand it being so cold, even in his car. Then they moved and I saw his face so I had to stay then, I had to stay and watch. I saw his face and

I saw hers just before he kissed her... Just before he did she looked like my Granny, old and tired and like she didn't care about anything at all anymore...

I stopped following him after that. I thought if he was with her he'd never come back to me and my Mum. Then I heard he was dead...

Pause.

I didn't know where to look for him then. I'm cold. Can I get a cup of tea or something?

Available in *First Run 3: New Plays By New Writers*, selected and introduced by Matthew Lloyd and published by Nick Hern Books. Reprinted by kind permission of the publisher.

ISBN: 1 85459 059 6.

GOODNIGHT CHILDREN EVERYWHERE

by Richard Nelson

Goodnight Children Everywhere was first performed at The Other Place, Stratford-upon-Avon, by the Royal Shakespeare Company in December 1997.

Spring, 1945. Evacuated to Canada five years earlier, 17-year-old Peter returns to London. His parents have been killed in the war, and his three sisters – Ann, Vi and Betty – eagerly await his arrival. But the family is a maelstrom of complex emotions.

Nineteen-year-old Vi (who was evacuated to Wales with Ann) is struggling to become an actress. Ann and Peter strike up a relationship which is more intimate than is appropriate for a brother and sister. Peter tells Vi, who responds by talking about another act of betrayal.

Accent: middle-class English.

VI: The ship after yours – the next ship carrying boys and girls to Canada – was torpedoed by the Germans and sank. They wouldn't let anyone – go after that. You were the last. (*Beat.*) We waited a full week wondering what had happened. If it had been your ship. (*Beat.*) We thought then we might have lost you. I even imagined, sitting in the bath, what it would have been like, felt like – to drown. And to float to the bottom of the sea. Like a leaf, I thought, as it falls. We cried ourselves to sleep. (*Beat.*) The first newspaper accounts said that the little boys had stood in perfect lines, all straight, all calm. Some could get into boats, some couldn't. Calm. Betty said that surely meant you couldn't be on that ship, our little Peter couldn't ever stand still. (*She smiles at Peter, then:*) For a week we held our breath. And then we heard. You were in Canada. You were lucky. How we celebrated! Mum and Dad and Betty and Ann and me. How happy we were that our Peter was safe. I'd never known a happier day. (*She picks up the photo again.*)

I began to dream you were coming home. (*Beat.*) Then, finally, you really were coming home. (*She sets the photo back down.*) Now you're home. (*She stands, calls.*) Betty, I'll help you with that dress!

She exits.

Available in *Goodnight Children Everywhere*, published by Faber & Faber Ltd. Reprinted by kind permission of the publisher.

ISBN: 0 571 19430 8.

ARCADIA

by Tom Stoppard

Arcadia was first produced at the Royal National Theatre in April 1993.

The play is set in an English country house in Derbyshire, both in the present day and in April 1809. In 1809, Thomasina Coverly, the daughter of Lord and Lady Croom, is 13 and intellectually precocious. Here, she is talking to her handsome young tutor, Septimus Hodge. Thomasina is studying a sheet of paper, a Latin 'unseen' lesson. She is having some difficulty.

Accent: upper-class English.

THOMASINA: *Solio insessa… in igne…* seated on a throne… in the fire… and also on a ship… *sedebat regina…* sat the queen… the wind smelling sweetly… *purpureis velis…* by, with or from purple sails… was like as to – something – by, with or from lovers – oh, Septimus! – *musica tibiarum imperabat…* music of pipes commanded… the silver oars – exciting the ocean – as if – as if – amorous –*regina reclinabat…* the queen – was reclining –

Is it Queen Dido? Who is the poet? Known to me? Mr Chater?

I know who it is, your friend Byron.

Mama is in love with Lord Byron.

It is not nonsense. I saw them together in the gazebo. Lord Byron was reading to her from his satire, and mama was laughing, with her head in her best position. She is vexed with papa for his determination to alter the park, but that alone cannot account for her politeness to a guest. She came downstairs hours before her custom. Lord Byron was amusing at breakfast. He paid you a tribute, Septimus. He said you were a witty fellow,

and he had almost learned by heart an article you wrote
about – well, I forget what, but it concerned a book
called *The Maid of Turkey* and how you would not give
it to your dog for dinner.

*SEPTIMUS returns her homework to her. She looks into
the book*

Alpha minus? Pooh! What is the minus for? You did not
like my discovery?

You are churlish with me because mama is paying
attention to your friend. Well, let them elope, they
cannot turn back the advancement of knowledge.
I think it is an excellent discovery. Every week I plot
your equations dot for dot, *x*s against *y*s in all manner of
algebraical relation, and every week they draw
themselves as commonplace geometry, as if the world of
forms were nothing but arcs and angles. God's truth,
Septimus, if there is an equation for a curve like a bell,
there must be an equation for one like a bluebell, and if
a bluebell, why not a rose? Do we believe nature is
written in numbers? We do. Then why do your equations
only describe the shapes of manufacture? Armed thus,
God could only make a cabinet.

We must work outwards from the middle of the maze.
We will start with something simple. (*She picks up an
apple leaf.*) I will plot this leaf and deduce its equation.
You will be famous for being my tutor when Lord Byron
is dead and forgotten.

(*Of the unseen.*) Is it Cleopatra? – I hate Cleopatra!
Everything is turned to love with her. New love, absent
love, lost love – I never knew a heroine that makes such
noodles of our sex. It only needs a Roman general to
drop anchor outside the window and away goes the
empire like a christening mug into a pawn shop. If
Queen Elizabeth had been a Ptolemy history would have

been quite different – we would be admiring the
pyramids of Rome and the great sphinx of Verona. But
instead, the Egyptian noodle made carnal embrace with
the enemy who burned the great library of Alexandria
without so much as a fine for all that is overdue. Oh
Septimus! – can you bear it? All the lost plays of
the Athenians! Two hundred at least by Aeschylus,
Sophocles, Euripides – thousands of poems – Aristotle's
own library brought to Egypt by the noodle's ancestors!
How can we sleep for grief?

Available in *Arcadia*, published by Faber & Faber Ltd. Reprinted
by kind permission of the publisher.

ISBN: 0 571 16934 1.

PART TWO: TWENTIES

HENCEFORWARD

by Alan Ayckbourn

Henceforward was first performed at the Stephen Joseph Theatre in the Round, Scarborough in July 1987, and subsequently in London.

The play is set in the future where violence on the streets has escalated to such an extent that certain areas of London have become no-go areas, controlled by marauding girl gangs. Jerome is a reclusive composer, who has hired Zoe – an escort – for personal services. Zoe is an attractive girl in her twenties but has just been attacked by one of the marauding gangs. Her clothes are in ribbons, her face is bleeding from a cut and her hands are torn and filthy. She has lost one shoe and is holding the other. Her stockings are in shreds. She obviously started out looking quite elegant in her smart suit and crisp blouse. This is her first meeting with Jerome.

Accent: English.

ZOE: I'm sorry. (*Brightly.*) Well, here I am. At last. (*She laughs nervously.*) What a super room.

Pause. She nervously indicates a seat.

Is this – for sitting on? Well. Would you mind if I – ? Thanks very much.

She sits. She gives a sudden, quite unexpected, reflex sob as the shock begins to take hold, but elects to continue as if it hadn't happened.

I'm sorry if I'm looking a bit of a – I must do a bit. I'm sorry. Anyway, I understand this was just an initial interview. Mrs Hope-Fitch told me you just wanted to look at me. See if I was suitable. But I believe the actual job's not for a week or so? Have I got that right? (*She sobs.*) Excuse me. Yes?

(*Indicating herself.*) Look, you'll just have to disregard all this. I mean, *this* is ghastly. But I can – you may not believe this – I can look pretty good. Although I say it myself. Yes? But as I say, not – don't, for God's sake, go by this. (*Sobs.*) Sorry.

Would you like me to – walk up and down? Give you an overall picture? People sometimes find it helps them to – get a more general… Of course, I don't quite know what you're looking for so it's a bit… I understand it was slightly unusual? Is that so? (*Sobs.*) I'll stand up. (*She does so.*) There.

Five foot four and a bit. I can lose a bit more weight if you like. I'm a bit over my usual… (*She sobs.*) I'll walk about for you. In case you need me to walk. (*She walks about, limping slightly.*) By the way, I don't usually limp, of course. Please disregard that. I just seem to have bashed my knee – anyway. And, naturally, with heels on I'm that bit taller. They help no end, of course, with all sorts of things. God, look at my legs. Don't look at those, either. I'm sorry, I'm afraid you're just going to have to take my word for an awful lot of things. (*She sobs.*) Look, I'm awfully sorry, I think I'm just going to have to go away somewhere and have a quick cry. I'm sorry, I'm just in a bit of a state. I am sorry. Is there a – ? Have you got a – ? I'll be as quick as I can. I'm so sorry.

Available in *Alan Ayckbourn: Plays 1*, published by Faber & Faber Ltd. Reprinted by kind permission of the publisher.

ISBN: 0 571 17680 1.

CROSSFIRE

by Michel Azama
(translated by Nigel Gearing)

Crossfire was first produced in France in 1988. This English translation was first produced by Paines Plough at the Traverse Theatre, Edinburgh in August 1993, and subsequently in London.

This is a non-naturalistic play about war and war atrocities. It interweaves time, place and generations in a seamless epic and poetic narrative. We know little of the specific backgrounds of any of the characters – often, they are archetypes.

Bella is 20 and a freedom fighter. In this scene she is talking to 15-year-old Ismail, her prisoner from the opposing side. War has thrown them together. Bella is tough and cynical beyond her years, accustomed to violence and not afraid of it.

Accent: any.

BELLA: He was called Yossif.

He was more than just a mate. Haven't talked about him for a long time.

When he went off to war I said to myself don't be so melodramatic.

All the women in this country think the same bullshit as you're thinking at this moment… then their men come back.

One day I get a postcard. I'm happy to see his handwriting. But then silence and more silence.

I couldn't imagine him killing anyone. What about you – have you killed anyone?

Right. What was I saying?

I wrote every day no answer. Then one Friday two men in plain clothes at the door. I stuffed my hand into my mouth and bit into it. He'd died February fourth and already been buried two days. I didn't cry. They gave me some water and I looked at the glass shaking in my hand.

It's afterwards it gets tricky. That same evening I asked a friend to take me out. I had to get out. We walked round town. It was curfew. I wanted to say, 'Take me in your arms. Touch me.' I didn't dare. He wouldn't have understood. I don't like you looking at me when I talk about it.

I bumped into one of my girlfriends – we were kids together. It turned out she'd been a war-widow for six years. I wanted to scream. I swore I'd never get like her. I'm not some monument to the dead. I know some who've gone mad. So – then and there – snap out of it, no more moping. My dresses my make-up my jewelry. The pain down here that's nobody's business. Every night I dream I'm dead. It helps.

It's funny. I've always had very simple problems that got complicated the longer I didn't deal with them. Problems with love, of affection, all that stuff. I'd like a good dose of sex to make me forget it all.

Available in *Crossfire*, published by Oberon Books Ltd. Reprinted by kind permission of the publisher.

ISBN: 1 870259 34 3.

THE TREATMENT

by Martin Crimp

The Treatment was first produced at the Royal Court Theatre in April 1993.

New York in the present day. Anne is a young woman in her twenties. She is on the run from her husband, who has kept her locked in their apartment. In Manhattan, two film producers – Andrew and Jen – offer to buy her story, but want to change it significantly. Here she is in Andrew's apartment, telling him how this experience feels for her.

Accent: New York.

ANNE: If he could see me here he would kill me. It's so hot in my hotel room I take endless showers. There's no bathroom *in* the room so I have to cross the corridor to the shower. The curtain is rotting, especially at the bottom where it's permanently damp, there's a kind of black mold growing on the blue plastic and people've left scraps of soap which I use to wash because I'm permanently shattered in this heat and I forget my own. So I take a shower with the scraps of soap then it's back to my room. I throw myself down on the bed and just lie there drying off in the current of air from the fan which I keep on maximum. For the first time in my life, my whole life, I'm completely free and alone and I can't bear it.

She drinks.

I've never traveled out of this *state* and yet I think I must be somehow jetlagged because I can't sleep but
I can't really wake up – is that what it's like? I just go from the shower to the bed and back to the shower again and my thoughts are in a loop: how I replied to the ad never thinking anything would happen – then there was the call and the limo arrived – it was so *long* and white and cool inside and the driver never met my eyes – then

you listened to my story and we went to the restaurant
where I must have made such a fool of myself knowing
nothing about anything, what to *order*, how to use
chopsticks, nothing, what to *say* to you, and I reply to the ad
and the call comes, and the limo comes, and I tell my
story, and we go to the restaurant and I just lie there
staring at the fan which is like a person a disapproving
person shaking its head going 'no no no I don't believe
this can be you Anne no no no no no no no no...'

*As she chants 'no no no...' she moves her head slowly from side to
side in imitation of the fan, her eyes shut. She opens her eyes. She
moves away, sipping the drink.*

I've escaped from the man who silenced and humiliated
me. So why does it feel like I'm betraying him?

Available in *The Treatment*, published by Nick Hern Books.
Reprinted by kind permission of the publisher.

ISBN: 1 85459 240 8.

SABINA!

by Chris Dolan

Sabina! was first produced by Borderline Theatre Company at the Cumbernauld Theatre in February 1998, prior to a major Scottish tour.

The play is set in Glasgow during the days leading up to the Velvet Revolution in Czechoslovakia in 1989. Sandra, a young woman from Maryhill, Glasgow, shares a flat with a Czech refugee, Tereza. Initially as a joke, the ebullient Sandra (an expert linguist who is learning Czech from Tereza) decides to pretend to be a Czech freedom fighter, Sabina Vasiliev, to test her theory that men are attracted to 'romantic' middle-European women. Her imposture is successful but, as matters proceed, Sandra begins to find her life as 'Sabina' more 'real' and appealing than her true identity. Tereza is outraged at Sandra's actions and reveals to Matthew, Sandra's new boyfriend, that 'Sabina' is a fraud. Sandra, left alone, is completely engaged in her alternative personality. It is the dead of night. Sandra wanders round the room.

Accent: Glaswegian impersonating Czech.

SANDRA: Ceskoslovensko. Skotsko.

> *Pause.*

At home, when I was young, I used to play by the stream in the garden of the River's Kiss. When it got dark, Maminka used to tell me stories. We sat by the water, and her voice washed over me like a wave. She told me the story of Snowflake.

Once upon a time it was wintery winter, all over the world. And in this winter there was a little girl – just like you, Sabina. The little girl had no-one to play with, so she made herself a friend – a snowgirl. She made her out of the cold, lifeless snow. She gave her long, white, snowy hair, and an icy sparkling dress. And she named her new friend Snowflake.

But then, when she made delicate lips of ice on her snowfriend, the little girl stood back, startled. Did she feel warm breath on her hand? Then Snowflake moved. She shook the loose snow from herself, and held out her hand. She was so pretty, and kind and gentle, that the little girl soon lost her fear.

All winter long, the little girl played with her new friend, whose eyes were as blue as the sky, and her words rang out bright and clear like crystals.

And around the little girl's cottage, so sad and silent for many years, there now echoed the happy chimes of the two friends' laughter.

And then the thaw came.

She looks at the gun in her hand. Brings it up to her face. Opens her mouth, points the gun inside. After a moment, she pulls the trigger.

And that was the end of the story.

Available in *Sabina!* published by Faber & Faber Ltd. Reprinted by kind permission of the Peters, Fraser & Dunlop Group on behalf of Chris Dolan.

ISBN: 0 571 19590 3.

THE POPE AND THE WITCH

by Dario Fo
(translated by Ed Emery)

The first production of this play, in the original Italian, was at the Teatro Lirico, Milan in January 1990.

In Dario Fo's characteristically quirky, irreverent and farcical style, the play tackles serious themes with iconoclastic exuberance. The Pope is sick. The second nun, who stands accused of being a witch, has been brought to the Vatican to effect a cure. She is not, in fact, a nun at all. She comes from Burundi. Here, she is speaking to a professor and a cardinal. Her age is not specified by the author.

Accent: any.

SECOND NUN: Watch who you're calling a witch, Cardinal, or I might just turn nasty. I'll turn you into a baboon, and you can wear your little red bobble hat on your baldy backside.

I shall go back to my drug addicts. At least they show a bit of gratitude… Not like some people I could name… We work wonders there. The Council were just on the point of shutting me down. The professor took advantage of this fact to do a bit of blackmail on me.

That's what I said – blackmail. He came to visit me, and more or less told me: 'Listen, I can save you. I can stop them evicting you, you and your drug centre, and throwing you all out into the street like they did the Leoncavallo centre… I can also help you to escape a prison sentence for serious professional misconduct… In exchange, however, I want you to do me a favour. The Pope is sick. I want you to come to the Vatican with me and see if you can use your hypnosis to cure him. Take it or leave it.'

Forget it, Professor. I can't say I've got a lot of time for His Eminence… The man's got no style…

(*She looks around for an ashtray. She doesn't find one so she passes her cigarette stub to the cardinal.*) I wouldn't want to desecrate the Holy See… Anyway, His Eminence is right… As Cardinal Biffi put it so nicely, we women are dismal creatures… advisors of the Devil, and propagators of death! The best thing we can do is just pull the chain and disappear from history. Goodbye.

Available in *The Pope And The Witch*, published by Oberon Books Ltd. Reprinted by kind permission of the publisher.

ISBN: 1 870259 58 0.

KEEPING TOM NICE

by Lucy Gannon

Keeping Tom Nice was first performed by the Royal Shakespeare Company at the Almeida Theatre in August 1988.

Tom is approaching his twenty-fifth birthday. He is severely handicapped and, in spite of the intervention of the social services, has lived in the care of his parents, who have devoted their lives to him. The family is now at breaking point.

Charlie, 23, is Tom's sister. She is at university and lives away from home. She went to university late after working in an office and taking her A levels at night school. She was desperate to make it to university to please her father and 'make up' for Tom. She is bright, apparently loving, but immature. In this scene, she rounds on her mother about the 'neat' way Tom is kept.

Accent: any.

CHARLIE: What is it you're so afraid of, you two? You are, aren't you? You're afraid of something.

Are you afraid that someone will be able to look after Tom as well as you do? Or better? Is that it? It is, isn't it? You want to be the only ones. The holy ones. Dedicated angels. Don't you? You make me sick.

You smooth the bed. You hang flowered wallpaper in his room, you feed him mush when the doctor told you years ago to let him *chew*.

I'm angry because you leave him in here while you watch the TV in there – because all he ever gets at Christmas is a pair of socks. One year a towel. A towel! All wrapped up in Santa Claus paper. But most of all I'm angry because you never, ever kiss him! I have never seen you kiss him. Hold him. In all the years – never! Oh, not now so much, not when he's a grown man, but then. I remember kissing him. How I used to sneak into his room and slide into bed with him, and whisper to him, silly jokes and childish stories – we grew up together but I got all the kisses and he got, what? Soapy flannels? Passive exercises.

He needed those things but not only. Not only! (*Softer.*) Oh, how could you *not* kiss him? His soft, sleeping body. His long, thin limbs. The curve of his eyelashes against his bed-warmed cheeks. For Christ's sake, Mum, whatever happened to him it happened inside you. That should draw you together, shouldn't it? He looks at you as if you were a God. A shining, breathtaking God. You know he does, don't you?

Available in *Keeping Tom Nice*, published by Warner/Chappell Plays Ltd. © 1988, 1990 by Lucy Gannon. Reprinted by kind permission of Warner/Chappell Plays Ltd, London. All rights reserved. Applications for amateur performance rights should be addressed to Warner/Chappell Plays Ltd at the address on page five.

ISBN: 0 85676 146 X.

THE AWAKENING

by Julian Garner

The Awakening was first staged at the Hampstead Theatre, London in April 1990.

The play is set in Norway, between the wars. On an isolated island, Unn, in her mid-twenties, has the sole running of the farm she owns jointly with her brother, a fisherman. In this scene, she is talking to Johannes, a prisoner in his mid-twenties, who is serving a life sentence for raping and murdering an eight-year-old girl. He has a slight mental handicap which has rendered him, in the author's description, 'tuppence short of a shilling'. Johannes had been in solitary confinement for two years until Agnes, a prison reformer, found him a job as 'slave labour' on Unn's farm. Unn has been teaching him farm work and has grown quite fond of him, though her manner remains stern. He works hard. This sensitive scene shows the beginnings of a relationship which will eventually become sufficiently tender for Unn to bear his child. Her reactions to his touch, and the feelings they awaken inside her, are at least as important as the words she speaks.

Accent: any regional accent.

UNN: Are you thirsty? Would you like something to drink?

JOHANNES looks at her.

Come.

They go into the kitchen. UNN gives him a glass of milk, he drinks. UNN takes out the Bible from the drawer of the table and gives it to JOHANNES. He reads to himself. UNN cleans the fish.

Have you ever seen Spring on a farm, Johannes? Just wait until you see the animals when we let them out. Especially the bulls. They're scared at first; we have to lead them out. It's so long since they saw daylight. But once they're used to it, you have to keep your distance, then! They kick their legs and bellow and jump about. Like fat men at a barn dance, who've had too much to drink.

JOHANNES laughs. Pause.

I think we must try to take you fishing again. It's nothing to be afraid of. The boat's steady as a rock and you're never more than a stone's throw from the shore. Johannes, you have to take over the fishing, sooner or later. April's a hard month.

She takes his hands.

Remember the first time you used an axe, how blistered your hands were? But they soon hardened up, didn't they, and now you can chop wood all day, if you like, your hands are used to it. It's the same with your stomach. It'll soon get used to a few waves.

She lets go of his hands.

You can be out with me, tonight. I'll show you how to set the nets. If you're still sick after a week you can stop. But you must try it for a week, at least.

She stares at her hands.

Johannes…

Don't call me Ma'am. Agnes used to call my mother 'Ma'am'. Call me Unn.

Yes.

Available in *First Run 3: New Plays By New Writers*, selected and introduced by Matthew Lloyd, published by Nick Hern Books. Reprinted by kind permission of the publisher.

ISBN: 1 85459 059 6.

SHAKERS: RE-STIRRED

by John Godber and Jane Thornton

Shakers: Re-Stirred was first produced by the Hull Truck Theatre Company in 1991. It is a revised version of a 1984 play, *Shakers*.

The play is set in Shakers, *a glitzy, trendy cocktail bar with pretensions to class in a city centre, somewhere in the UK. The cast of four actresses each play cocktail waitresses, and also role-play various customers. The style is broad and up-front comedy for much of the play, but every so often each of the waitresses steps forward to share her deeper feelings with the audience. Carol is one such waitress, in her twenties.*

Accent: any.

CAROL: I can't help it, I hate it when people just assume that because you do a job like this, you're thick. You know there's some nights I just can't stand it. I can't. I want to stand up on top of the bar and shout: I've got O levels, I've got A levels and a Bachelor of Arts Degree. So don't condescend to me, don't pretend you feel sorry for me and don't treat me like I can't read or talk or join in any of your conversations because I can. I see these teenage-like men and women with their well-cut suits and metal briefcases, discussing the City and the arts and time-shares in Tuscany, and I'm jealous, because I can't work out how they've achieved that success. It's so difficult. You see, I want to be a photographer, take portraits. I won a competition in a magazine. It was this photo of a punk sat in a field on an old discarded toilet. It was brilliant. Anyway, after college I had this wonderful idea that I'd go to London with my portfolio. I was confident that I'd get loads of work. But it wasn't like that. The pictures were great, they said, but sorry, no vacancies. My mum said I was being too idealistic wanting it all straight away. My dad said I should settle for a job with the local newspaper,

snapping Miss Gazette opening a shoe shop. No thanks.
Now he thinks I'm wasting my degree. I was the first in
the family to get one so it's not gone down very well.
My head's in the clouds, he said, life's not that easy. But
it is for some people, like I said, I see them in here. So
why should I be different, have they tried harder or
something? Maybe they're lucky or it's because they
speak nice. It's frustrating because I know how good
I am. My dad's right, you know, in some ways: I'm stuck
here, wasting away. I do it for the money, that's all. But
it won't be forever, no chance. I'm applying for assisting
jobs, and as soon as I get one, don't worry, I'm off. I'm
now on plan two: start at the bottom and work up. It
might take me years, I know that, but it's what keeps me
going between the lager and the leftovers. The fact that
I know I'll make it in the end.

Available in *Shakers: Re-stirred*, published by Warner/Chappell
Plays Ltd. © 1987, 1993 by John Godber and Jane Thornton.
Reprinted by kind permission of Warner/Chappell Plays Ltd,
London. All rights reserved. Applications for amateur
performance rights should be addressed to·Warner/Chappell
Plays Ltd at the address on page five.

ISBN: 0 85676 166 4.

SHAKERS: RE-STIRRED

by John Godber and Jane Thornton

See note on the play on page 41.

Nicky, a cocktail waitress in her twenties, has just got a job dancing on a cruise liner. At the start of the speech she is talking to her fellow-waitresses, then to the audience.

Accent: any.

NICKY: Think of me in a month's time, the lights, the roar of the greasepaint, the smell of the crowd. I've always wanted to do it and at last I'm giving it a go.

(*To audience.*) I know they're jealous of me. I don't blame them, no-one wants to stay here. It's funny though now I can escape, I'm bloody scared to death. Nine months, it's a long time, what if I don't make any friends? What if I get seasick, or food poisoning, or lost somewhere in a forest and have to live with a tribe of eskimos and never come home again? I know I'm being stupid. My mind's gone haywire. But deep down I'm a panicker, I can't help it, but in reality it's frightening leaving it all… your mum, your dad, your mates. I'm excited as well though, don't get me wrong. I wouldn't forego the opportunity, it's a chance in a lifetime: travel, freedom, celebrity. Oh yeh, I've definitely got to go! But the actual job? I wouldn't tell the others but more than anything I'm apprehensive about that. I've got to lose some weight for a start, some of the costumes are ever so small, sequins and all that stuff, but there is some topless as well. It's classy, it's all part of the dancing. But it's getting over that first time, isn't it? Then I'm sure I'll be alright. You see to be honest it took me about four days to get them out when we went to Ibiza and then I laid on my front. I suppose though they're alright, even if I'm not Bridget Nielson. And they did look at them so if they were awful they wouldn't have had me. Like I said I'm sure I'll get used to it. It's all the excitement, it makes you nervous I don't know black from white. But I'm sure it will be brilliant, I'm sure it will. I mean the world will be my oyster, I can't believe it! That's the thing though isn't it? What do you do when a dream comes true? What do you dream of then?

ISBN: 0 85676 166 4.

AMY'S VIEW

by David Hare

Amy's View was first produced at the Royal National Theatre in June 1997.

The play concerns the troubled mother-daughter relationship between Esmé, an actress, and Amy, her daughter, over a twenty-year period. In this scene, set in 1979, Amy is just 23 and has found herself to be pregnant by her boyfriend, Dominic. She is described as 'dark haired, in jeans and a T-shirt, she is thin, with an unmistakeable air of quiet resolution'. Amy is speaking to her mother.

Accent: middle-class English.

AMY: The truth is… my relationship with Dominic has been pretty fragile. It's volatile, is that the word? He can be bad-tempered. He suffers from depression quite badly. At times he… well, he's like… he's a victim of moods.

So the point is, I thought, this is really tricky. Do I just go to him and tell him outright? No, that's going to shock him. And also… I know for a fact he will say to me, look, will I get rid of it? And, for me, there's no question of that. So, alright. It's like solving a puzzle. I want to keep the baby and I want to keep Dominic as well. So I must work out a way of telling him so he doesn't feel pressured, so he doesn't feel, 'oh God, this is just what I feared…'

He said… he has said from the start he wasn't ready for children. He said this. From the very first day. The point is, I made him a promise. No children. He said: 'Whatever else, I can't face starting a family…' (*She stops a moment.*) So you must see that does make things difficult now… Because I just know – I can feel in my stomach – it's going to seem like it's blackmail. For him it'll be like I'm springing a trap. (*She suddenly raises her voice.*) It's everything he feared! I know him. You don't.

I tell him now and at once he's going to feel cornered…
and when Dominic feels cornered, I tell you, I've seen
him, he turns just incredibly stubborn and ugly…

Mother, I'm sorry, but I'm very clear about this. (*She is
reluctant, not wanting to go on.*) The fact is… you know…
I'd not wanted to tell you… the girl who was with him
before… the point is she also… she also got pregnant.

Oh look, I mean it's not… it wasn't immediate. It wasn't
like, 'She's pregnant, I'm off…' But it's true. He stopped
her having the baby. Then he told me things did start to
sour between them. And, pretty soon after, he felt that
he'd had enough.

I know… I know, Mother. I know what you're going to
say. But the answer is: yes. He is the right man for me.
I know this. I know it profoundly. In a way which is way
beyond anything.

So it's just a question of what I do now.

Available in *Amy's View*, published by Faber & Faber Ltd.
Reprinted by kind permission of the publisher.

ISBN: 0 571 19179 7.

THE COMMON CHORUS

by Tony Harrison

The Common Chorus was first published in 1992.

The play is a version of Aristophanes' classic comedy Lysistrata *but it is set at Greenham Common during the 1980s when the Women's Peace Camp was at its most active. As in the Greek original the women have refused to sleep with their men until peace is restored.*

Lysistrata, in her late twenties, the leader of the women, is confronting a government official.

Accent: any.

LYSISTRATA: We've heard you men plan world-wide
                                          Apocalypse
  and we went on serving dinner with sealed lips.
  We went on sitting with our knitting in our laps
  while you moved model missiles on your maps.
  We heard the men's low murmur over their moussaka
  and knew the world's future was growing a lot darker.
  Serving the coffee we heard dark hints
  of coming holocaust with after-dinner mints.
  All this time, supportive to the last,
  we nailed our colours to your macho mast.
  I tried to discuss it with my husband, tried
  to say he shouldn't vote for national suicide.
  O hello darling, did you vote Yea or Nay?
  'Me, I'll always vote for Cruise to stay.
  What's it got to do with women anyway?
  Your province is knitting not national defence.'
  A man of sense alright, if you can call
  sense wanting to destroy us all.
  But male misgovernment grew more crass
  and in the end we women couldn't let it pass.
  Crasser and crasser, week by bloody week.
  We could have told you if you'd let us speak.
  You've set the world on a collision course
  and still go on believing in masculine brute force.

We were finally driven out by sheer desperation
to devise a strategy to save the nation.
Perhaps it was the day we heard recruiters cry
that able-bodied men were in short supply.
And we decided there was no point waiting
for men to end the war when it was escalating.
If men didn't want to staunch the flow of blood,
there was no choice about it, we women would.

Available in *The Common Chorus*, published by Faber & Faber
Ltd. Reprinted by kind permission of the publisher.

ISBN: 0 571 14723 2.

THE WOMAN WHO COOKED HER HUSBAND

by Debbie Isitt

The Woman Who Cooked Her Husband was first performed by the Snarling Beasties Company at the University of Warwick in 1991 and subsequently transferred to the Royal Court Theatre in London in October 1991.

Kenneth and Hilary have been married for a long time but, with middle age approaching, he finds himself in the arms of another woman, Laura. But Laura can't cook, and Kenneth starts vacillating between the two. The play is blackly comic and explores jealousy, humiliation, deceit and betrayal in an original and exuberant way.

Hilary, the deserted wife, is preparing a meal for Laura and Kenneth – a meal neither of them is likely to forget.

Accent: any.

HILARY: (*She is singing* Stardust Melody. *She notices the audience and stops, as if taken by surprise. She stands behind the table. To the audience.*) The kitchen is a murderer's paradise. Saucepans crack, knives chop, scissors stab, matches burn, microwaves electrocute, kettles of boiling water scald – the possibilities are endless – especially when you have an axe to grind.

It's funny really – considering we spend most of the time in the kitchen – why is it male murderers often want to cook their victims – I'm surprised they know how. But me – I'm an expert cook. I can disguise anything – the times I've served up yesterday's remains and with a little bit of this and a little bit of that – called it by a French name and fooled my husband into thinking he was eating something truly fresh and exotic. Well, food – like sex – is all in the mind.

Kenneth went to great lengths to encourage my interest in everything culinary. Well naturally, husbands want their wives to be good and careful cooks – their very health depends upon it. But how foolishly they trust, these men – how lacking in suspicion. How many wives have pondered poison while stirring in the gravy, then backing down at the last minute, just spat in it instead – it's food for thought though, isn't it?

It has taken me a long time to discover that even though I'm single and have been for many years, I'm still not free. I am suffering from the ex-wife syndrome, a bleak vision of the future has overtaken me – an image of myself growing old, alone, loving no-one ever again. I am plagued by fantasies of him making love to her – still, now – I'm upset that he looks good, been able to move on with his life, because, when I look at myself in the mirror, I see an image of a woman who doesn't measure up, one who has been banished to the sidelines and replaced. I see nothing more than Kenneth's ex-wife.

Since the day he left me, obsessive thoughts have been slipping in and out of my mind, shocking, morbid ideas. That day, I was mincing some meat for my dinner and I had a spark – what would it be like to mince his flesh – would he make a good steak or a better bolognaise – he's such a beefy man – not just skin and bone – he's really meaty – I can just smell the garlic on his breath – it's enough to frighten anyone to death.

Available in *The Woman Who Cooked Her Husband*, published by Warner/Chappell Plays Ltd. Reprinted by kind permission of Warner/Chappell Plays Ltd, London. All rights reserved. Applications for performance rights should be addressed to Warner/Chappell Plays Ltd at the address on page five.

ISBN: 0 85676 163 X.

THE WOMAN WHO COOKED HER HUSBAND

by Debbie Isitt

See note on the play on page 49.

Laura is Kenneth's second wife and the biggest problem in their marriage is that she cannot cook as well as his first wife, Hilary. It has awoken other feelings of inadequacy in Laura. Laura is speaking to the audience.

Accent: any.

LAURA: I really didn't know I was capable of such thoughts, it's terrible really – the way they creep up on you when you least expect them – murderous thoughts, cheap and nasty. If only Hilary would disappear – Ken couldn't find so much fault with me – no Hilary to compare me with. If only Hilary wasn't here – Ken would have to eat my meals – without Hilary we could be happy – it's just with her still – around – it makes that hard – a constant reminder of how good things were, how clean things were – how well cooked things were – how well ironed – how neat and how tidy – how I wish that Hilary would have an accident – nothing really horrible like a car crash but maybe roll under something like a bus – instantly squashed – feeling no pain – like a rabbit on a road at night – splat – all over – non-existence – snap my fingers – gone – not there – 'Where's Hilary, I wonder. I popped round to see her and the place was deserted. Perhaps she's run off with a business tycoon' – that would serve him right – but I can't see it happening overnight. I know it's wrong – God help me, I know – I just can't help thinking how much easier I'd feel. No shadowy woman lurking in the past ready to pounce on me at any minute and tell me what I've done to her and how happy she made Ken.

I must stop this soon, it leaves a nasty taste in your
mouth – I mean, what's she ever done to me? I never
thought I'd be like this over a man. I've always thought
of myself as independent and free. It shouldn't matter
what he thinks – I shouldn't let him rule my days – I'm
sorry God for what I said about Hilary – she deserves
a break – it's just that I don't think I can cope with life –
being such a useless wife.

Available in *The Woman Who Cooked Her Husband*, published
by Warner/Chappell Plays Ltd. Reprinted by kind permission
of Warner/Chappell Plays Ltd, London. All rights reserved.
Applications for performance rights should be addressed to
Warner/Chappell Plays Ltd at the address on page five.

ISBN: 0 85676 163 X.

A PRAYER FOR WINGS

by Sean Mathias

A Prayer for Wings was first performed at the Edinburgh Festival in August 1985 and was subsequently seen at the Bush Theatre in London.

The play is set in Swansea, South Wales. An old church has been poorly converted into a dwelling. Rita, a plain girl of 20, lives here in poverty with her sick mam, who suffers from multiple sclerosis and with whom Rita has a complicated relationship. She longs to get away. Mam has just gone to sleep, and Rita addresses the audience.

Accent: South Wales.

RITA: Now I could do it. Do her in. Finish her off. I'd take that pillow and hold it over her head. She's got no strength in that small body of hers. Hardly any fight in them arms. The struggle wouldn't even be noticeable… except… I suppose if they examined her insides, her lungs would be all funny. I suppose it wouldn't look like she'd just passed on in her slumbers. Still, I could run away. Go to a really big city. Go to a really big country. Meet a man. A real man. We'd go out dancing. Go to the cinema. Posh restaurants. And he wouldn't try to interfere. He'd be a real gent. He'd pop the question. On bended knee. I'd say 'Yes. Yes, Boy, I'll have you, to have and to hold, in sickness – God save us – and in health, to our dying day. I'll cook and I'll wash. We'll have our own machine. And I'll give you babies, four boys, lovely little boys. And they'll grow up to be captains. Captains of their teams. Captains of their generations. And we'll be old and comfortable and proud of our boys. Our four boys.' And there'll be no smelly grandparents to have to answer to.

(*To MAM.*) Mam? Are you asleep? Sleeping, Mam?

There's a bad smell in here. A definite bad smell.
I think Mam's started farting. Call this life?

Mam! Settle down, love. I can hear your shuffling.

(*With growing intensity.*) Wishing and wishing and
wishing and wishing and wishing and wishing and
wishing and wishing!

Available in *A Prayer For Wings*, published by Amber Lane
Press. Reprinted by kind permission of the publisher.

ISBN: 0 906399 77 7.

MISHA'S PARTY

by Richard Nelson and Alexander Gelman

Misha's Party was first produced by the Royal Shakespeare Company at the Pit in the Barbican in July 1993.

The play is set in Russia on 20 August 1991, the night of an attempted coup against President Mikhail Gorbachev's government. In the Ukraine Hotel in Moscow, Misha is giving a sixtieth birthday party for himself, insisting on the presence of his two ex-wives and their new partners, his daughter and her flatmate – Lydia, who is also Misha's fiancée. Lydia is 25. Misha's family and friends believe that he is dying, though he is not. Furthermore, Lydia has just discovered that Misha has been having an affair with her friend, Raya. Here, in the early hours of the morning, with riots outside the hotel, Lydia confronts Misha in the lobby of the hotel. She calls him by his given name – 'Mikhail'.

Accent: any.

LYDIA: Mikhail.

I wanted to see you. I wanted to see you alone. (*Beat.*) Are you alright?

Mikhail. I want you to know that I have known about you and Raya since the morning after it happened. Everyone knows, Misha. You slept with her. Perhaps still are sleeping with her. I'm not sure about that. Mikhail, Masha told everyone, please! I am not criticising you, I knew about it. These things happen. I understand. (*Beat.*) I wish Masha had kept it to herself, but… I simply wanted you to know that that wasn't the reason. Do you want a drink?

She takes out a small silver flask.

I was going to give this to you. Why not, I still will. Here.

She hands him the flask.

Happy birthday. I think everyone else has forgotten it – was – your – birthday.

Sits down.

I suppose it was when we thought – everyone thought you were dying –

Let me finish. This is very important to me. (*Beat.*) When I started to believe about your imminent death, something happened to me, Mikhail. Something that I will admit is quite selfish – which as you know is very rare for me. Anyway – what I started to do – was think about – me. And then you came into the restaurant. I looked at you – or I remember thinking I was looking at you – very very differently. (*Beat.*) What struck me – I saw you for the first time as a dying man – what struck me was – that you are old. Sh-sh. Please. Old. I'm just about finished. A dying old man. That's what I saw and I can't erase what I saw from my brain now can I? It's how I saw you – it's how I see you still. (*Beat.*) Because – you *are* old, after all. I just hadn't seen that before. I'm sorry.

She takes off her ring and hands it back to him.

I really am sorry. And I want to apologise for my selfishness. It's not often in my life that I have thought of me. If you wish I won't tell Raya right away about us. This. I think – intrigue excites her.

By the way, of course I'm happy you aren't dying – and I'm sure most of us feel that way.

Available in *Misha's Party*, published by Faber & Faber Ltd. Reprinted by kind permission of the publisher.

ISBN: 0 571 17117 6.

THE NEIGHBOUR

by Meredith Oakes

The Neighbour was first produced at the Royal National Theatre in April 1993 as part of the Springboards Festival.

The play is set on a London council estate in the 1990s. Liz shares a flat with her brother, James, and his partner, Stephi. She is unemployed and tends to stay close to home. In this scene, set in the flat, she is speaking to Stephi about her pet mice, Eddy and Freddy. Liz has just made them a woollen pom-pom for their cage.

Accent: London.

LIZ: Look what I made for Eddy and Freddy. (*She holds up the pom-pom.*) Do you want to see me give it them? (*Goes to the cage of Eddy and Freddy.*) Hullo Freddy darling, you in your wheel are you? Oh, the little love, he's a little muscle mouse. Where's your friend? Where's Eddy? Look at him, you can see his little mind going round. Eddy? Eddy? Come and see what Liz has got. Something nice and soft for you. (*To STEPHI.*) Who was that in the car with him? Was that Celestine, was it? (*To mice.*) Oh yes, ain't you a strong little mouse, you can spin that great big wheel all by yourself. Mind you don't catch your tail, that's what happens to little boys who show off. Eddy! I don't know why Eddy won't come out. (*To STEPHI.*) You won't see James till morning then.

He's a law unto himself though, ain't he, you'll never change him. I could never change him. I never had the slightest control. He was such a lovely-looking little boy though. (*To mice.*) Oh yes Freddy, you're a lovely-looking little boy too, you've got a lovely pink nose and it's ever so pointy. Go and get Eddy for me. Go on. (*To STEPHI.*) I hope Eddy's alright. He might be sick, mightn't he. I ought to take off their roof and see what he's up to.

LIZ takes the roof off the cage.

Look at you, you sleepyhead. Don't you want to see what I got for you? Come on, I thought you was supposed to be nocturnal. Here, what you got there? Show Lizzie. Oh! It's a baby! It's a tiny little baby. Fancy that.

Eddy ain't a little boy, he's a mother.

Did you ever see anything so tiny? It looks like it's made of jelly, don't it, like something from the sweet shop. It's like a jellybaby with hands.

LIZ reaches into the cage.

(*To STEPHI.*) I'm only going to put it next its mother. Eddy won't mind, Eddy's my baby, ain't you darling. (*To mice.*) Where's it gone, Eddy, where's your little baby? Look behind you, stupid thing. She's Edwina now. Oh blimey, look at that, will you? She's eating it. Horrible little creature! Horrible little thing! Eating it! Her own baby!

I shouldn't have touched them, it's against their instincts ain't it. You told me not to touch them. You mustn't disturb them, must you. That's what they say. I got what was coming to me, didn't I? But it's unnatural, ain't it? I shan't give them that pom-pom now. It'll go straight in the bin.

Available in *The Neighbour*, published by Oberon Books Ltd. Reprinted by kind permission of the publisher.

ISBN: 1 870259 31 9.

THE EDITING PROCESS

by Meredith Oakes

The Editing Process was first performed at the Royal Court Theatre in October 1994.

The play is a satire about a small publishing company taken over by a major London publishing house. Eleanor, 22, is the niece of the owner of the large company. She has been in publishing for six months. She does not get paid but thinks it will 'lead to a position'. She has been appointed editorial assistant to Footnotes to History *and in this scene is talking to William, the ageing editor of* Footnotes.

Accent: upper-class English.

ELEANOR: I never see my uncle. My uncle despises me. He's despised me since I was born. He despises mummy. He's got granny's corner cupboard, it was the only thing in my grandparents' house that mummy really wanted. Granny said it was going to be mummy's, but when they got back to the house after the funeral, mummy discovered it was gone. Afterwards she found he'd got it in his flat.

Was it valuable? What difference does it make, I despise possessions. That's why I particularly can't understand a person wanting to take them away from me. Because it would have been mine, mummy said.

That's what's so stupid, he's willing to make us all hate him for the sake of a corner cupboard. I can't stand my family, they have no sense of proportion. I'd rather throw myself into a volcano than be like him.

He couldn't care less if I'm right for this job, the reason I've got this job is, I haven't got the corner cupboard.

Please don't ask me to phone him, it makes me feel unclean. I'm going to wash my hands.

Available in *The Editing Process*, published by Oberon Books Ltd. Reprinted by kind permission of the publisher.

ISBN: 1 870259 46 7.

THE EDITING PROCESS

by Meredith Oakes

See note on the play on page 59.

Tamara del Fuego, 29, is a corporate image consultant who has been brought in by a major London publishing house to give the image of their latest acquisition 'a radical reassessment'. She prides herself on being exotic and 'arty'. She is talking to Eleanor, a rather colourless young Sloane Ranger, whose uncle runs the company.

Accent: upper-class English.

TAMARA: Do you want to see your new letterhead? It's gorg. (*ELEANOR looks.*) Go on, tell me you love it, it's a mock-up obviously, the editor's name goes there, we can put that in later to avoid any uncertainty. Isn't it beautiful.

That's exactly what I was aiming for, timeless is the next big thing. What's your game plan, Eleanor? When I was your age I had the next ten years mapped out. Well I still am your age.

Sometimes I think what I do is actually therapy, you know? Helping companies through a crisis of identity? Because there's no such thing as a bad company. We're talking a confused company, with myself as the medium through which this company can be released. The company talks to me and I listen. I help the company to express what was previously perhaps too obvious for anyone to mention. When I encourage a company to create its new corporate image, that's like a rite of passage for that company, it achieves a deeper awareness of what it want to project, and I give it the tools it needs to define itself. So it becomes a sort of celebration, a coming of age or a wedding feast, where money should be no object. Should it.

Anyway Lionel told this company I'd be mega. They're
not expecting the Seven Wise Virgins. Hostess to
a concept is what I am. Well of course the company's
given me a budget and I've totally overspent it, and
I think everyone should feel they've had a wonderful
blow-out and that it's a really special time. I mean
I hope your uncle will understand. Perhaps you could
have a talk with him. If you're interested, the girl who
does my office is having a baby and I'm going to
have to replace her, I didn't realise I was harbouring
a breeder, I don't pay much but it isn't about pay,
ultimately, is it?

Don't think your uncle's going to do anything for you,
the owner only uses him for getting into clubs. Don't
stay too long, this company's dodgier than eggs. Yes,
I'm transforming its fortunes with a new corporate
image. I am. This company's going to die with a smile
on its face.

Available in *The Editing Process*, published by Oberon Books
Ltd. Reprinted by kind permission of the publisher.

ISBN: 1 870259 46 7.

PENTECOST

by Stewart Parker

Pentecost was first performed in the Guildhall, Derry, by the Field Day Theatre Company in September 1987 and was subsequently produced at the Lyric Theatre, Hammersmith.

The play is set in Belfast in 1974. Ruth is 29 and has been married for 10 years to a violent husband, David. David is a policeman in the Royal Ulster Constabulary. She has left her husband three times before, but always gone back to him. Now, in the early hours of the morning, she has turned up at the new home of Marian, her childhood friend. Ruth is talking to Marian throughout this speech.

Accent: Belfast.

RUTH: It's quite hard, getting here. That fire's quite warm. I know it's a bit late to be asking, I would have phoned only you haven't got one, I did actually phone, at the flat, and the shop, not knowing, but anyway – if there was any chance, you could maybe put me up for the night. Marian. I have decided, actually. To leave – David.

I'm not making excuses for him. He's not a bad person, Marian, honest to God, his nerves are frayed away to nothing…

They never know the minute, he's had three good mates killed in his own station, and a fourth one blinded, it's the waiting around all day that gets to him, all the threats and the hatred and no outlet, he comes home coiled up like a spring, he's frightened of his life, it's all pent up inside him… Christ, I'm no better, sitting at home, waiting to hear the worst… I caught my sleeve on one of his swimming trophies – Waterford crystal it was – it smashed to bits in the hearth… I just stared down, stupid, at the pieces like a child who knows it's in for

a thumping… it was a sort of blinding crunch and a flash
of light. I was lying behind the sofa then and I could feel
my hair getting wet… twice more he hit me… but I had
my arms up by then… the phone started to ring. I think
that saved me, not that he answered it, it sort of half
brought him round, he just stared down at me and said,
'that's you sorted out', and then he threw the truncheon
into a corner and went into the hall for his coat and
I heard the front door slamming. He hadn't even had
his dinner. So I got up and cleaned myself off – I knew
then I had to go, get away – I didn't want to be there
when he got back, not this time – I really knew this
time I couldn't live with him anymore – how can
you love somebody once you're actually in fear of
your life of him – I don't blame him, Marian, but
I can't stay with him, I can't stand being so scared…
I'm sorry.

Available in *Three Plays For Ireland*, published by Oberon
Books Ltd (out of print). Reprinted by kind permission of
the publisher.

ISBN: 1 870259 17 3.

I AM YOURS

by Judith Thompson

I Am Yours was first presented by Tarragon Theatre, Toronto in November 1987 and by Shared Experience at the Royal Court Theatre in February 1998.

Mercy has come to visit her sister, Dee, who she finds is pregnant. Both women are disturbed by their past experiences. In this scene, Mercy has just heard Dee tell the father of her child that she wants nothing to do with him and will give the baby away.

Accent: American or Canadian.

MERCY: That was a hideous thing to do. That was a disgusting, cruel, horrific…

No, no, this time I will not get off your case.

You make me sick you are so smug and beautiful, you have no idea what it is to be me, all the boys looking straight at you, never at me. That time at the dance when you went straight up to Stephen Gilroy who you knew was crazy about you and said, 'Oh dance with Mercy, she loves you so much.' And the other time in front of all our friends when you made me pick my nose and eat it; you said I had to, to get in your club, that you'd all done it. And then I did it. And you laughed, you laughed. Do you know how much I hated you? Do you know how much?

If you're a woman and you're born ugly you might as well be born dead. Don't. Don't you laugh.

Don't put down television, you snot, television has saved my life. It has literally saved my life, when you're so lonely you could die. I mean shrivel up and die because nobody cares whether you get up or stay in bed or don't eat, when you're so lonely every pore in your skin is

screaming to be touched, the television is a saviour. It is
a voice, a warm voice. There are funny talk shows with
hosts who think exactly like I do. And when the silence
in your apartment, the silence is a big nothing and
you're thinking, my God, my God, is this what life is?
Years and years and years of this? You turn on the
television and you forget about it. Often all I'll think
about all day at work is what's on TV that night,
especially in the fall, with all the new shows, I get really,
genuinely excited. I... I love television. I love it. It
makes me happy so don't put it down.

Available in *I Am Yours*, published by Faber & Faber Ltd.
Reprinted by kind permission of the publisher.

ISBN: 0 571 19612 8.

I AM YOURS

By Judith Thompson

See note on the play on page 65.

Dee is a disturbed young woman, frightened by her own capacity for violence. As a result of this fear she has separated from her husband and now finds herself pregnant by the supervisor of her apartment building. She opts for an abortion. In this scene, Dee has left her pre-surgery bed and wandered down the halls, in her gown. She has felt the life of the foetus inside her and cannot go through with the abortion. She addresses the audience as if it is the foetus.

Accent: American or Canadian.

DEE: A feeling like a push; somebody strong, pushing me off the table, it was not a … decision, I was pushed and I felt and I feel and I hear… a breathing… inside me, that is not my own. I do… hear it. A raspy kind of sweet breathing a – a – pulling for breath, for air and kind of a sigh of content. I feel the breath on my face the drops of wet breath, hear a sigh, are you there? A voice not mine, a voice like no other; there you are, in the sighing, and I know I think I know whose voice this is; this is yours, this is yours, this is not a mirage, no, not part of the madness, a moment of clear, oh yes, you are clear, I can taste your sweet breath, a flower, not mine, not mine but inside me I can feel on my hand the press of your hand, fingers, holding my hand, tiny fingernails, not letting go, the impression, the feel of a tiny body lying next to mine, breathing, in the bed, cream sheets. I am asleep; how can I see this? How? You are showing me, showing me, you are looking at me with your dark blue eyes, staring at me in the dark in the night, smelling my milk, breathing fast for my milk, the shininess of your eyes like the moon on the water I see: I see it, in my mind, too clearly, just as I can hear your voice, too too clear, rising, falling, your eyes, looking at me from across the room, watching me move across the kitchen, watching me; when I hold you and you wrap your hair around your tiny hands, pulling, and your head on my chest rooting for the breast, I can hear, I can feel the rooting. I am lost, I have heard you, I can feel you drinking of me, you drink my milk and you drink and you drink and, oh, I am lost.

Available in *I Am Yours*, published by Faber & Faber Ltd. Reprinted by kind permission of the publisher.

ISBN: 0 571 19612 8.

PART THREE: THIRTIES

MAN OF THE MOMENT

by Alan Ayckbourn

Man of the Moment was first performed at the Globe Theatre, London in February 1990.

The play is set on the paved pool/patio area of a modern, moderately sized villa in a Spanish-speaking area of the Mediterranean, owned by former criminal and now TV personality, Vic Parks. Jill Rillington, in her early thirties and looking good – certainly at first glance – is every inch the assured, charming TV reporter/presenter. This is the opening moment of the play. She is doing a piece to camera, though, Ayckbourn comments, we won't guess this immediately.

Accent: any.

JILL: (*To camera.*) Hallo. I'm Jill Rillington. In this edition of *Their Paths Crossed*, we tell a story that started 17 years ago in the slow and sneet of a Surrey Novem… Oh, piss! Keep rolling. We'll go again. Snow and sleet. Snow and sleet… (*Slowly.*) Snow – and – sleet… Here we go. Snow and sleet. Hallo. I'm Jill Rillington. In this edition of *Their Paths Crossed*, we tell a story that started 17 years ago in the snow and sleet of a Surrey November morning, and finishes – (*She gestures.*) here. In the brilliant sunshine of a glorious Mediterranean summer. It's a story which has – fittingly perhaps – almost a fairy tale ring to it. A tale with a hero and a villain – even a damsel in distress. But this is no child's fable, it is a true story. This is the real world where nothing is as it seems. This is the real world where heroes are easily forgotten; this is the real world where the villains may, themselves, become heroes. And as for distressed damsels – well, are they in reality ever truly rescued? I'll leave you, the viewer, to judge for yourself…

She pauses for a moment, looking towards the camera.

And – cut! OK? Did you get the wide? (*Gesturing.*) The wide?

Good. Did you get this whole area? (*Gesturing and yelling.*) This whole area?

What? (*She notices her radio mic.*) Oh, yes. Sorry, Dan. Didn't mean to burst your eardrums. Sorry, my love. (*She consults her watch. She makes to yell again then thinks better of it.*) George – (*Quietly.*) Sorry, love. Dan, can you tell George to set up the arrival shot. For the arrival. Can he do that? Where we talked about? On the bend? So we see this man's taxi coming up the hill and their first meeting at the front door? OK? George knows where. I'll be with you in a sec. Thank you, love. I'll unplug. Save your batteries.

Available in *Alan Ayckbourn: Plays 1*, published by Faber & Faber Ltd. Reprinted by kind permission of the publisher.

ISBN: 0 571 17680 1.

THE MAI

by Marina Carr

The Mai was first produced at the Peacock Theatre, Dublin in October 1994.

This is a memory play. Thirty-year-old Millie looks back on her 16-year-old self and her family at their house on the shores of Owl Lake, in the Irish Republic. The 'Mai' of the title is Millie's own mother, Mai, who at times seems almost like a creature from mythology. In an effort to escape her mother's emotional clutches, Millie has turned her back on home and family. Now, with the Mai dead, she has returned to the house by Owl Lake to confront her ghosts.

Accent: Irish.

MILLIE: Joseph, my five-year-old son, has never been to
Owl Lake. I thought of having him adopted but would
not part with him when the time came, and I'm glad,
though I know it's hard for him. Already he is watchful
and expects far too little of me, something I must have
taught him unknown to myself. He is beginning to get
curious about his father and I don't know what to tell
him. I tell him all the good things. I say your Daddy is
an El Salvadorian drummer who swept me off my feet
when I was lost in New York. I tell him his eyes are
brown and his hair is black and that he loved to drink
Jack Daniels by the neck. I tell him that high on hash
or marijuana or god-knows-what we danced on the roof
of a tenement building in Brooklyn to one of Robert's
cello recordings.

I do not tell him that he is married with two sons to
a jaded uptown society girl or that I tricked him into
conceiving you because I thought it possible to have
something for myself that didn't stink of Owl Lake.
I did not tell him that on the day you were born, this
jaded society queen sauntered into the hospital, chucked

you under the chin, told me I was your Daddy's last walk on the wild side, gave me a cheque for five thousand dollars and said, you're on your own now, kiddo. And she was right. I had no business streelin' into her life, however tired it was. I do not tell him that, when you were two, I wrote a sensible letter, enclosing a photograph of you, asking him to acknowledge paternity. And I do not tell you he didn't answer.

Available in *The Mai*, published by The Gallery Press Reprinted by kind permission of the author and The Gallery Press.

ISBN: 1 85235 161 6.

DEAD MAN'S HANDLE

by John Constable

Dead Man's Handle was first published in 1997, after being performed by the Soho Theatre Company.

This is a short play set beside the bed of a man on a life-support machine. The woman, whose age is unspecified by the author, is in shock. As she sits beside the man's bed, she speaks her thoughts to him, and we gradually learn more about their relationship. At the start of the speech, she adopts a breezy, innocuous tone.

Accent: any.

WOMAN: Sorry I'm late. Took me forever to get here. Incident on the Piccadilly Line… You won't believe this – they had a runaway tube train! Driver gets out to check the door. Train pulls out, rattles on through the next station. So then, of course, the whole system grinds to a halt while they check the line. We were stuck in the tunnel for over an hour. By the time we got out it was in the late edition.

She opens her evening paper, scanning the report, as if keeping up to date with the news.

Apparently it's technically possible for trains to move without the driver – although the brakes are supposed to engage automatically if the driver's handle – it's funny, they call it the 'dead man's handle'… is… released.

Her voice trails off. She throws down the paper, gets up and lights a cigarette, pacing around the bed, distractedly taking several drags before she realises she's smoking in a hospital.

Oh God – what am I doing?

She stamps out the cigarette.

Be just like me to go and set off the alarms.

She sits back down, staring at the MAN. Pause.

Hello… It's me. Remember? Are you there? Hello? Anyone there? You always think somehow there'll be… time… to say the things you… And then it's too late… No-one to hear it…

Pause

Listen! I don't want to lose you. But, to see you like this… reduced to… I know. It's selfish… I say to myself "For *your* sake. I don't want you to suffer" – but what I mean is, "*I* don't want to *see* you suffer." I just… can't bear this… dead weight of seeing someone I love slowly wasting away before my eyes. I want to close my eyes and picture you as I knew you, with all your faculties intact. But this… This isn't you. Is it? If they could heal you, somehow… restore you, make you whole again… But if they can't, I wish… I wish they'd just let you…

Pause. She takes his hand.

I had a dream about you.

Available in *John Constable: Sha-Manic Plays*, published by Oberon Books Ltd. Reprinted by kind permission of the publisher.

ISBN: 1 870259 90 4.

SILLY COW

by Ben Elton

Silly Cow was first performed at the Theatre Royal, Haymarket in February 1991.

This comedy centres on the repellent Doris Wallis, queen of the tabloid press who is, in her own words, 'a nasty cow who slaughters sacred cows'. Described by the author as 'bitchy, brassy and bolshie' she is every inch as unpleasant as the public persona she so carefully cultivates. In this scene Doris is due to be interviewed on Wogan, *a TV chat show. She is speaking to Sidney, a tabloid newspaper man who 'likes to think of himself as a rough diamond' and who has been trying to persuade Doris to sign a contract with him.*

Accent: any.

DORIS: Well, pardon me if I don't chew your trousers off and kiss the great man's bum. I've said I'll probably take the job and I really don't see why I should have to sign anything.

I just have a problem with signing things, that's all. I think I must have been scared by a contract as a small child.

Of course I trust you, Candyfloss. I trust all editors to be dirty, duplicitous little weasels and not one has ever failed me. You're not the only one who'll be giving things up, Sidney Skinner! You're not the only one who's had to work hard for everything they've got. While you were sneaking around Hollywood trying to buy photos of Jackie Onassis with her fun bags flying, I was dogsbody on the *Preston Clarion*, and I mean dogsbody.

Yes, and I'm never going back. These last few years I've finally got a grip of *la dolce vita* and I'm sticking my talons in deep. I am never again going to get up at five-thirty on a rainy morning to report on a sheepdog trial,

I am never again going to cover the Liberal candidate in a by-election, and I am never again going to review another show at Preston Rep.

There was this appalling old ham; I'd watched him every three weeks for two-and-a-half years, and whatever part he played, he did his Noël Coward impression. Hamlet's ghost, Noël Coward. *The Crucible*, Noël Coward, *Mother Courage*, Noël Coward. Imagine what the old fart was like when he actually had to play in a Noël Coward – his accent got so clipped I swear he was only using the first letter of each word. So please believe me, Sidney, I am never going back to that. I've done my time, Sidney, and now it's paying off. I've got my own column, I've cooked with Rusty on TV-AM, two *Blankety Blanks* last series, and Les called me Cuddles. What's more, tonight is the big one, I get my first *Wogan*. These are not things you throw away lightly, Sidney. Which is why I am just a little bit hesitant about ending up in Stuttgart working for an editor I scarcely know… I don't like being pushed around and I certainly wouldn't dream of signing anything without showing it to Peggy. If Peggy thinks it necessary, she'll show it to a lawyer. Anyway, it'll have to do. I'm not going to change again.

Available in *Silly Cow*, published by Warner Books. Reprinted by kind permission of the author.

ISBN: 0 7515 0190 5.

THE SECRET RAPTURE

by David Hare

The Secret Rapture was first produced at the Royal National Theatre in October 1988.

Katherine, in her early thirties, is the wild and alcoholic widow of Robert Glass, a much older man. Robert's daughters are older than she is. At the funeral, and immediately afterwards, Katherine is drinking and throughout this speech has the out-of-focus logic and self-pity of the alcoholic. She is talking to Isobel and Marion, Robert's daughters, and Marion's husband, Tom.

Accent: English.

KATHERINE: I've spoken to Mrs Hurley. I was in the kitchen. Lunch will be ready in three-quarters of an hour. She's planning a rabbit and vegetable pie.

Tom appears. KATHERINE smiles.

I outsmarted him. I've hidden the bottle again.

Now KATHERINE is suddenly emotional, the alcohol flowing round in her and coming out as tears.

It gives me confidence, and I must say today I should be allowed a little confidence. Given what lies ahead.

She smiles bravely, wiping her eyes with her sleeve. She sits down.

Your dad never told you, he actually met me when he stopped one night in a motel. It was in the Vale of Evesham, he was coming back from the North. I don't know how I'd ended up there. I was working the bar. It was appalling. Trying to pick men up – not even for money, but because I was so unhappy with myself. I wanted something to happen. I don't know how I thought these men might help me, they were travellers, small goods, that sort of thing, all with slack bellies and smelling of late-night curries. I can still smell them,

I don't know why, I'd been doing it for weeks. Then Robert came in. He said, 'I'll drive you to Gloucestershire. It will give you some peace.' He brought me here, to this house. He put fresh sheets in the spare room. Everything I did, before or since, he forgave.

She sits, tears in her eyes, quiet now.

People say I took advantage of his decency. But what are good people for? They're here to help the trashy people like me.

(*To MARION.*) The ring you gave Robert is missing. Yes. Today I went into his room. I was planning to give it to you. The funny thing is, I guess you'd already taken it.

Available in *The Secret Rapture*, published by Faber & Faber Ltd. Reprinted by kind permission of the publisher.

ISBN: 0 571 15408 5.

SKYLIGHT

by David Hare

Skylight was first produced at the Royal National Theatre in October 1994.

Kyra is just past thirty, described as 'quite small, with short hair and a practical manner'. She comes from a privileged background but now works as a teacher in a tough inner-London school. She is speaking to Tom, 20 years her senior, and her former lover. They have not met for three years. Kyra had once lived with and been part of the household of Tom and his wife, Alice, but left immediately Alice discovered the affair. Tom is a successful businessman, running a chain of restaurants. Here, Kyra recalls how she first met Alice and, through her, Tom. Kyra is talking to Tom and cooking as she speaks.

Accent: any.

KYRA: I was a waitress for 45 minutes. Alice made me the boss on the spot.

It was my first trip to London, I just walked in off the street… I was so thrilled, I remember. At last I'd escaped. I was walking down London's famous King's Road. I saw the sign 'Waitress Wanted'. I walked in. Alice told me I could start right away. Then after an hour of it, she came running over. She said her daughter was in hospital, she'd fallen off her bike. She said she'd looked round and she'd decided. Could I run the place for the night?

I said, 'I've only just started, I only started an hour ago.' She said, 'I know. I've watched you. I trust you. Now you must trust me, you're going to be fine…' Oh it can't have been later than eight o'clock. I mean, oh yes, I handled it. I know I did the whole thing. Then I closed up. All the waiters were great, they were really great considering I'd only just arrived yet I was in charge.

They all said, 'Look, we promise, there's really no need
for you to hang on here. Just lock up the door and we're
all going home…

She has left the cooking and is now standing at the kitchen door.

But I don't know… I just had this instinct. Somehow
I didn't think it was right. I can't quite explain it.
I wanted to be there when Alice got back. It's funny. Of
course, I would have met you anyway. Surely I would
have met you the next day. Who knows? But there was
something about that evening. Something to do with the
evening itself…

She looks away absently.

I sat alone. Drank expresso. Smoked cigarettes. I'm not
sure I'd ever sat through a night. This deserted restaurant
all to myself. But filled with inexpressible happiness.
This crazy feeling. 'I don't know why but this is where
I belong.'

And then… Need I continue? Then towards morning she
came back with you.

Available in *Skylight*, published by Faber & Faber Ltd. Reprinted
by kind permission of the publisher.

ISBN: 0 571 17612 7.

FAITH

by Meredith Oakes

Faith was first performed at the Royal Court Theatre Upstairs in October 1997.

The play is set in a remote island farmhouse at a time of war, 1982. A group of English soldiers are fighting for possession of the island. Nothing in their training prepares them for this situation. They have billeted themselves with Sandra, a farmer's wife in her thirties. She is talking to the soldiers, whose presence she resents, during this scene.

Accent: any regional accent.

SANDRA: The spring here is beautiful. It's beautiful with the sun shining, and the wind blowing the grass all up the hillsides and the quiet in the valleys. The little flowers are amazing... Sea pinks along the headland, daisies, there's actually a daisy that smells like chocolate, they call it the vanilla daisy... The air in this place is normally so clean, you notice the change when you get within a mile of town, you start smelling the petrol, that's how clean the air is normally. Normally you could go round the beaches and see elephant seals. The animals never learned the fear of man. God they must be thick. I have to get the dinner.

Think it's rubbish here don't you. Think we're rubbish. How you can make out you want to fight for us... you want to fight because you want to fight and that's all. And if we're rubbish... What are you? You're dossers. If you weren't doing this. You'd all be on the social. If it wasn't for all this. Where would you be? Living in some flat on some estate, and your biggest thrill of the day would be cutting your toenails with the breadknife. Dregs of society, you are. Get yourselves killed, best thing for everyone.

It's such a crying shame. That the opposite sex. Had to be men.

Available in *Faith*, published by Oberon Books Ltd. Reprinted by kind permission of the publisher.

ISBN: 1 870259 80 7.

COMMUNICATING DOORS

by Alan Ayckbourn

Communicating Doors was first performed at the Stephen Joseph Theatre in the Round, Scarborough in February 1994 and subsequently in London.

The play is concerned with time-travel and is set in the same hotel room in 2014, 1994 and 1974 respectively. In 2014, Poopay ('It's French for doll. La Poupée') is a prostitute, specialising in domination, who regularly works the five star Regal Hotel. She is described by the author as blonde, heavily made up, aged thirty plus but having a fair stab at twenty-five minus.

Poopay has been hired for an elderly client, Reece, but she finds, to her surprise, that he does not want sex. He wants her to witness his signature on a document and then deliver the document to a specific address. He believes he is being watched and his actions controlled. He has made a great deal of money out of shady deals in the past and wants to confess, particularly to the murder of his second wife, Ruella. In trying to persuade a reluctant Poopay to carry out his wishes, he has become confused, thinking her to be his daughter, Rachel. Then he has a heart attack.

Accent: English.

POOPAY: I am not Rachel! And I'm not getting involved. I'm sorry. I mean, if these people are happy to push women out of windows, what chance have I got? Most of your lawyers are bent as well, from the sound of it. I'm not having anything more to do with it, I'm sorry. You'll have to ask Quentin. Ask Rachel. You can leave me out. Ask Lennox. Anyone but me. I'm sorry. I'm getting my coat. No charge, alright…

For the last time will you stop calling me that? My name's not Rachel. It is Poopay Dayseer. Now, let go of me, will you…?

Get off! Off! Off! Alright? Or I'll break your stupid fingers. (*She prises him off her.*) That's better.

She starts to move away. The exertion has proved too much for Reece. He collapses, making strangulated noises.

What you doing now? What is it? What's the matter? What's the matter with you?

Reece lies on the floor making strangled breathing noises.

Oh my God! Oh, God! I'm getting out of here. I'm sorry, I'm getting out. Where's my coat? What's he done with my bloody coat?

She finds her coat and starts putting it on.

Look, I'm sorry about this. I'm making no charge. Alright? (*Grabbing her bag.*) That was on the house. I hope you're better soon…

She hesitates, then relents.

Oh God. Alright. Wait.

She puts down her bag and picks up the phone. She consults the notepad and works the phone.

I'll phone him. I'll phone your – your butler – whatever he is – then I'm away, alright? (*Into phone.*) Hallo… is that… whoeveritis…? This is Poopay… the – specialist consultant… in room – hang on a minute… (*She studies the phone.*) … What…? No, he's not – he's lying on the floor… he's had some sort of… hallo…

The phone has gone dead. Poopay replaces the receiver and grabs up her bag. Reece continues to lie on the floor, breathing with apparent difficulty.

(*To Reece, loudly.*) There's somebody coming. Can you hear me? There's somebody on their way. You'll be OK now.

Reece groans.

Oh, soddit. Here.

She grabs a cushion from the sofa and puts it under Reece's head.

I'm S&M, not doctors and bloody nurses… Right. Better?
Night, night.

Available in *Communicating Doors*, published by Faber & Faber
Ltd. Reprinted by kind permission of the publisher.

ISBN: 0 571 17682 8.

Also published by Oberon Books in association with LAMDA:

Contemporary Scenes for Young Men (1985-2000)
ISBN: 1 84002 141 1

Solo Speeches for Men (1800-1914)
ISBN: 1 84002 046 6

Solo Speeches for Women (1800-1914)
ISBN:1 84002 003 2

First Folio Speeches for Men
ISBN: 1 84002 015 6

First Folio Speeches for Women
ISBN: 1 84002 014 8

Classics for Teenagers
ISBN: 1 84002 023 7

Scenes for Teenagers
ISBN: 1 84002 031 8

Solo Speeches for Under 12s
ISBN: 1 84002 013 X

The LAMDA Anthology of Verse and Prose, Vol XV
ISBN: 1 84002 120 9

The LAMDA Guide to English Literature
ISBN: 1 84002 011 3

The Discussion
ISBN: 1 870259 71 8

Mime and Improvisation
ISBN: 1 84002 012 1

Meaning, Form and Performance
ISBN: 1 870259 74 2

Great Speeches from European Drama
ISBN: 1 84002 002 4